T · R · U · E

COLORS

Country Living

TRUE

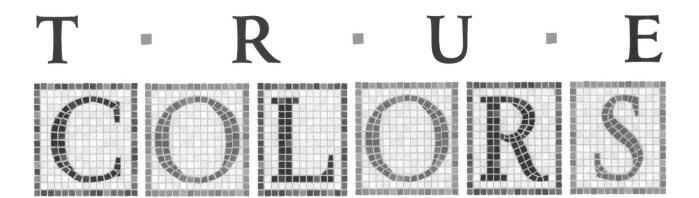

COLORS

Text by

D O N N A   S A P O L I N

Foreword by

R A C H E L   N E W M A N

H E A R S T   B O O K S

New York

Recognizing the importance of preserving what has been written, it is the policy of William Morrow and Company, Inc., and its imprints and affiliates to have the books it publishes printed on acid-free paper, and we exert our best efforts to that end.

Photography Credits appear on page 223.

Library of Congress Cataloging-in-Publication Data

Sapolin, Donna.
True colors / text by Donna Sapolin : foreword by Rachel Newman.
p. cm.
At head of title: Country living.
ISBN 0-688-15094-2
1. Color in interior decoration. I. Country living (New York, N.Y.)
II. Title.
NK2115.5.C6 26 1997
747'.94—dc20
96-42686
CIP

PRINTED IN SINGAPORE

FIRST EDITION

1 2 3 4 5 6 7 8 9 10

Country Living STAFF
Rachel Newman, Editor-in-Chief
Nancy Mernit Soriano, Executive Editor
Julio Vega, Art Director
Mary R. Roby, Managing Editor
Marjorie E. Gage, Features and Arts & Antiques Editor
Robin Long Mayer, Senior Editor / Decorating and Design
John Mack Carter, President, Hearst Magazine Enterprises

Editor LINDA HETZER
Designer SUSI OBERHELMAN

PRODUCED BY SMALLWOOD & STEWART, INC., NEW YORK CITY

CONT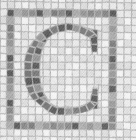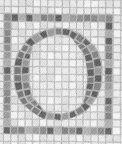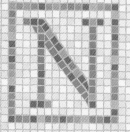

PALES

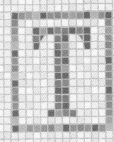
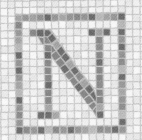

ENTS

DESIGN

FOREWORD

I came from an artistic family where shapes, forms and especially colors were thought of as tools of creativity. For me, bold use of color, like profound music and poetry can evoke emotional responses not easily described. My father, an artist, used lavish color in his impressionistic paintings. My mother filled our home with rich color in the form of textiles, pottery and cut flowers from her garden. I began to draw early and my parents encouraged me to let my imagination loose with my crayons . . . and later my tempera paints. Like most girls brought up in the country, I went through a horse-crazy stage and naturally I began to draw horses. But not content to color them realistic browns and tans, I made them blue, green, and purple. Later, as a teen-ager I was given the opportunity to choose a color to paint my bedroom. I chose a rich chocolate brown. Though warned by neighbors that it would be difficult to paint over, my parents gave me free reign to go with the brown. When I went off to college my mother presented me with a book called "The Language of Color." A book she had treasured as a child, she passed it on to me and it remains one of my treasured gifts. And so it was that color was an integral part of my creativity. My ability to combine or contrast color was far more advanced than my ability to draw. In my homes and apartments color became the unifying theme behind my disparate collections. But as I matured I learned that not every one felt confident about working with color. Many people fear making a mistake with color and end up with "safe" but uninteresting environments. Here at *Country Living*, we hear from hundreds of readers each year pleading for help with color selection for their homes. So it is in the spirit of our belief in the transformational qualities of color that we bring this book to you.

RACHEL NEWMAN

I N T R O D

COLOR IS THE MOST EXCITING, MOST POWERFUL, AND EASIEST-TO-USE OF
DECORATING TOOLS. IT NOT ONLY CONSISTENTLY EVOKES A RESPONSE
BUT IS AVAILABLE TO ANYONE, AND, WONDERFULLY VERSATILE, CAN BE
INTRODUCED INTO A ROOM IN AN INFINITE NUMBER OF WAYS — FROM
PAINT AND FABRIC TO DECORATIVE DETAILS THAT INCLUDE WALL-
PAPER, PAINTINGS, FURNITURE, ART, AND COLLECTIONS. NO DECORATIVE
INGREDIENT TRANSFORMS A SPACE WITH AS MUCH GUSTO AS COLOR; IT
TUNES THE HEARTS AND MINDS OF OCCUPANTS TO A PARTICULAR EMO-

U C T I O N

TIONAL PITCH AND RALLIES THEM TO A POINT OF VIEW. IT CAN BE

USED TO MANIPULATE THE SENSE OF SPACE IN A ROOM, MAKING IT

FEEL MORE AIRY, COZY, LARGE, OR SMALL; TO CREATE A PARTICULAR

MOOD — TRANQUIL, ENERGETIC, FORMAL, OR CASUAL; TO HARMONIZE A

RANGE OF OBJECTS; AND TO EMPHASIZE ARCHITECTURAL FEATURES.

INSPIRATION FOR COLOR CHOICES LIES ALL AROUND US: IN

NATURE, WITH ITS SUBTLE YET FAR-REACHING PALETTE OF NEUTRALS

AND PASTELS; IN THE TILE, WOODWORK, AND WALLS OF THE HOUSES

AND PUBLIC SPACES WE ADMIRE; IN OLD AND NEW SWATHS OF FABRIC;
IN COLLECTIBLES AND ARTWORK; AND IN ONE'S OWN REPOSITORY OF
VISUAL IMAGERY GATHERED OVER A LIFETIME OF LOOKING AND SEEING.

THE OPTIONS ARE VAST, BUT AN UNDERSTANDING OF THE COLOR
WHEEL, A UNIVERSAL DEVICE THAT SHOWS HOW COLORS FALL INTO THE
SPECTRUM, AND INSIGHT INTO CLASSIC COLOR SCHEMES CAN HELP GUIDE
APPROPRIATE COLOR SELECTIONS: THERE ARE THREE PRIMARY COLORS —
RED, YELLOW, AND BLUE; THREE SECONDARY COLORS — ORANGE, GREEN,

AND VIOLET, MADE BY MIXING EQUAL AMOUNTS OF TWO PRIMARIES;

AND SIX TERTIARY COLORS — YELLOW-ORANGE, RED-ORANGE, RED-VIOLET,

BLUE-VIOLET, BLUE-GREEN, AND YELLOW-GREEN, MADE OF A PRIMARY COLOR

THAT IS MIXED WITH AN EQUAL AMOUNT OF AN ADJACENT SECONDARY

COLOR. BLACK ADDED TO A COLOR CREATES DARK TONES OR SHADES,

WHILE THE ADDITION OF WHITE CREATES TINTS.

THREE BASIC DECORATIVE COLOR SCHEMES EMERGE FROM THE

COLOR WHEEL RELATIONSHIPS: AN ANALOGOUS OR MONOCHROMATIC

SCHEME USING COLORS THAT ARE ADJACENT ON THE COLOR WHEEL (FOR EXAMPLE, BLUE AND BLUE-GREEN) OR DIFFERENT SHADES OF THE SAME COLOR; A TRIADIC SCHEME, WHICH INCORPORATES THREE COLORS EQUIDISTANT FROM EACH OTHER ON THE WHEEL, SUCH AS YELLOW, RED, AND BLUE; AND A CONTRASTING OR COMPLEMENTARY SCHEME THAT USES COLORS OPPOSITE ONE ANOTHER ON THE WHEEL, KNOWN AS COMPLEMENTARY COLORS. COLORS THAT SHARE THE SAME TONAL VALUE, A TERM THAT DESCRIBES THE LIGHTNESS OR DARKNESS OF A COLOR,

GENERALLY WORK WELL TOGETHER. WHILE ALL OF THESE SCHEMES ARE CLASSIC DEVICES THAT PRODUCE HARMONIOUS AND ENGAGING RESULTS, IT IS IMPORTANT TO REMEMBER THAT THE APPLICATION OF COLOR TO A ROOM IS AN OPEN-ENDED ADVENTURE LIMITED ONLY BY THE EXTENT OF ONE'S IMAGINATION AND SENSE OF ADVENTURE.

TRUE COLORS AIMS AT ELIMINATING SOME OF THE GUESSWORK SURROUNDING THE APPLICATION OF COLOR BY STIMULATING THE IMAG-INATION AND SUPPLYING A PROFUSION OF SIMPLE DECORATING IDEAS

REVOLVING AROUND COLOR. THE FIRST PART OF THE BOOK PRESENTS

NATURAL AND PASTEL COLORS, TWO MUTED COLOR FAMILIES WITH THE

ABILITY TO ENLIVEN ROOMS WITH REFRESHING DELICACY. THE SECOND

PART EXPLORES FOUR BOLD COLORS — YELLOW, RED, BLUE, AND

GREEN — THAT LEND VIBRANCY AND DRAMA TO ANY SPACE, HOLD IT

IN THE GRIP OF EMOTION, AND PRODUCE POWERFUL VISUAL AND

PSYCHOLOGICAL EFFECTS. THE THIRD SECTION OF THE BOOK SHOWS

THE MEANS BY WHICH COLOR ENTERS AND ENERGIZES A ROOM: PAINT

AND THE MANY DIFFERENT WAYS IT CAN BE APPLIED; FABRIC; AND DECORATING DETAILS WITH THEIR SPECIAL TOUCHES.

By PROVIDING INSIGHT INTO THE CHARACTERISTICS OF INDIVIDUAL COLORS AND SHOWCASING THEIR IMPACT IN DIFFERENT SETTINGS ON A VARIETY OF MATERIALS, ARCHITECTURAL FEATURES, AND DECORATIVE OBJECTS, *TRUE COLORS* CONFIRMS WHAT A VITAL TOOL COLOR IS FOR SELF-EXPRESSION AND WHAT A STRIKING DIVERSITY OF LOOKS IS POSSIBLE FOR THE CREATION OF A WARM, INVITING, AND BEAUTIFUL HOME.

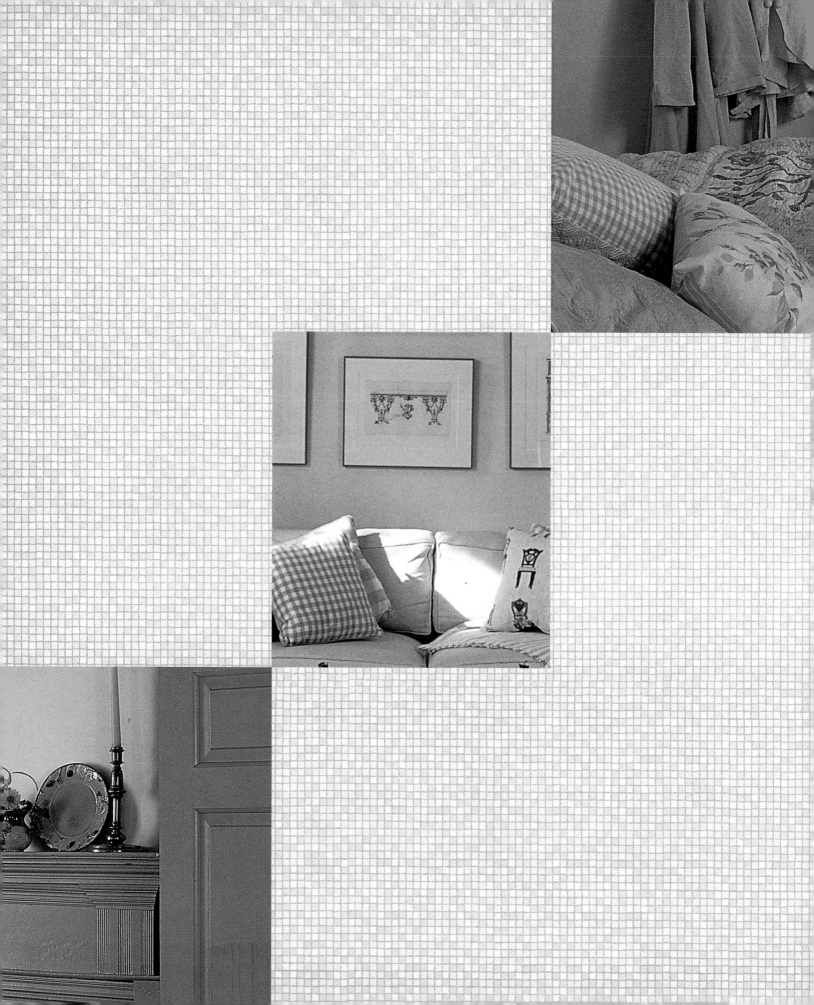

PALES

NATURALS

Naturals are the grays and tans, whites and creams, taupes, beiges, and browns found in nature — in clouds, stones and pebbles, earthen mounds, tree trunks, and branches. Each of these elements contains an abundance of distinct shades and nuances that radiate simplicity, serenity, and earthiness. A look at the white paint chips in a hardware store suggests the great variety of tones available in just one of the natural colors. Though muted and restful, naturals are never boring. Because they stem from nature, they are timeless decorative components that help balance the mood of an interior. Found indoors in the structure of a room as well as in furnishings and accessories — in wood posts and beams, stone fireplaces and walls, wood furniture, cane seats, sisal mats, wicker

baskets, earthenware jars, and nubby linens — naturals are full of intricate textures for the eye to explore. Because natural tones recede, they help richer colors look fresher and more lively. Naturals therefore make ideal background colors for rooms filled with bright accessories. Natural colors can also alter the perception of a room's size: A pale shade makes a ceiling seem higher; pale walls and furniture make it feel larger and less cluttered; brown tones, on the other hand, create a sense of warmth and enclosure, while grays lend depth and stateliness. A white hallway filled with greenery feels large and airy; a kitchen lined in wood feels cozy and welcoming. Naturals affect the amount of light in a room: Pale naturals reflect it; dark woody tones and grays soak it up. Natural hues defy the seasons: Whites evoke the coolness of winter no matter what the climate, while browns and creams wash a room in warmth. When wood is allowed to play off white in a room, the resulting balance between coolness and warmth, earthiness and purity, is soothing and visually interesting. Blends of naturals create subtly invigorating rooms that are comforting and inviting.

White wood furniture and old garden accessories grouped together on a stair landing (opposite) create a pleasing monochromatic color scheme. The warm wood staircase and ceiling beams add depth and definition to the cool white walls and furnishings and lend a sense of balance to the scene. Creamy white walls in a foyer (above) let warm wood furniture stand out, and they in turn give the light-filled entrance a cozy feeling.

A dining room (opposite) feels both open and contained because of the balance of naturals in the space. The knotty pine planks anchor the eating area in warmth and coziness. The upper, white portion of the walls reflects the light that pours in through the skylight and draws the eye up, accentuating the room's great height. An arched window links the upper and lower sections of the room with its pine trim. The pieced quilt on the balcony railing, featuring colors used elsewhere in the room, especially the soft blue of the distressed finish on the hutch, softens the effect of so much wood and adds more warmth to the room. In a kitchen (above), a monochromatic color scheme draws attention to the textures of the materials, and the patterns and colors of the decorative accents. In such a uniform color scheme, the eye searches out variety. Wood on every surface of the kitchen produces an even tone that allows each accessory — shiny earthenware crocks, framed vegetable prints, a woven basket, and vintage flour and sugar containers — to stand out. The painted green diamonds on the wood floor, reflecting the gentle green on the painted cupboard, anchor the room's many accessories.

A mix of woods and whites is a very effective manipulator of space. In an 1850 granary turned into a living and dining room (opposite), dark wood plank side walls and parchment-toned end walls emphasize the room's narrow shape and soaring height, while the rough-hewn beams overhead give the space a sense of enclosure. The white slipcovers enhance the feeling of light in the room, and their vertical stripes accentuate its height. In the sitting area of a large kitchen (above) furnished with white furniture and sofas, the whites never appear glaring or boring because of the layering of tones and textures: nubby oatmeal upholstery, a whitewashed wood fireplace screen and architectural decoration over the mantel, a white and natural woven basket, and pure white wool throws. The patina of the old wood floors and ceiling beams forms a frame around this study in naturals. In a living room (overleaf), loose-fitting white linen slipcovers, a pale wood floor, and pure white walls give the room an uncluttered contemporary feeling despite the presence of many historical details such as the dentiled cornice molding and the wood mantel, the antique hutch displaying earthenware jars, and the whimsical weather vane and quilt.

Gray, a pale version of black — a powerful neutral that conveys weight and solemnity — is a good choice for rooms in which a sedate natural color is desired. The soft gray in the walls and carpet of a living room (above) sets a dignified and restful stage — one that tempers the brightness of the white pieces but preserves their airy appearance. Although this gray is refined, it also allows for the light-heartedness of the decor — the bold stripes in the carpet, the painted wicker armchairs, and the bright yellow desk chair — and lets these elements add a note of vigor to an otherwise calm room. A deeper gray tone, such as that of the sofa in a family room (opposite), lends whatever it covers a stately character and is a good color for items that need to hold their own alongside vibrant accessories like the colorful quilt. Punctuated by the windows' cream fabric swags and moldings, the three shades of light gray on the walls tend to recede and therefore lend the sofa prominence. These grays also pick up the warmth of the nearby fabric colors because pale gray is a chameleon color.

CARVED IN STONE

Stone walls and fireplaces, built for centuries by farmers and homesteaders clearing their lands, evoke a country feeling and lend any room a sense of solidity. No two stones are truly alike; their mottled patterns are intriguing and draw the eye back again and again. And because they are usually a mixture of nature's neutral tones — grays, creams, beiges, and whites — stone walls make great backdrops for decorating schemes that emphasize that same family of neutral colors. They make the most of neutral furnishings by blending harmoniously with them while presenting a contrasting texture. White or cream furniture and walls let a dark stone fireplace stand out, while gray furniture allows beige stone walls to upstage it. Primary-color accents get even richer against stone's neutral tones. A floral fabric placed near stone re-creates a scene from nature because, like wildflowers growing alongside a riverbed, florals imbue stone with a sense of life.

A COLLECTOR'S HOUSE

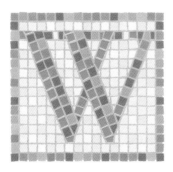

When a designer and avid gardener first purchased his Maryland home, a tiny two-hundred-year-old tollhouse, it was covered in unsightly brown paneling and built-in cupboards that made its cramped spaces seem even more congested and dreary. To turn the rooms into airy spaces that could show off the soothing, natural character of his furnishings — an abundance of green, white, and brown architectural and garden artifacts — he replaced the living room cupboards with old barn boards and painted these and all the paneling white. A self-described lover of spring who prefers cool natural colors to primaries, the homeowner counted on white's space-expanding quality to tie his collections together and lend his rooms a restful appearance.

After living with the white walls for a while, however, he felt that they looked too glaring and uninteresting, and rag-painted over them with a warmer white paint, a historical color diluted with water. This layering of white tones gave the walls an intriguing mottled look and a mellow glow that resembles faded old plaster.

The homeowner extended this paint treatment to the dining room walls, which were covered in a gray fake stone paneling. Against this subtle backdrop, a stunning collection of old green watering cans introduces indoors the tones of the homeowner's garden — a monochromatic panorama of all green plants and no flowers. The use of many naturals diffuses the sense of clutter in these rooms and accentuates the pleasing geometric forms of the objects in them.

To add depth to the living room without using bright colors, the homeowner placed several brown wood pieces and rusting accessories around a pair of pure white sofas and columns, and painted the floor in a high-contrast, brown and white checkerboard pattern. With its visual drama below eye level, the floor does not detract from the intrigue of the weather-beaten objects or the crisp, clean stage the white furnishings set. Since the surroundings never compete for attention with their

In the dining room (opposite), a parchment-colored wall supplies a natural backdrop for vines entwined around a column and a collection of old watering cans that stand at attention on a set of white shelves. An undulating panel of off-white fabric hung from a narrow rod gives the window poetic rhythm. The living room (overleaf) sets a tranquil scene for garden-oriented objects: a rare 1920s birdhouse with a copper roof, a pair of iron candelabra once used for outdoor weddings, and a wrought-iron patio chaise longue.

The bedstead (above) is made of branches that were cleared from a friend's property and painted white. Dressed in linens made of ticking, the bed introduces blue into an otherwise all-white room. The white bathroom (opposite) has become a garden with a sheathing of chicken wire on its walls and tub enclosure that supports delicate tendrils of miniature ivy.

contents, it was easy for the owner to weave in the fascinating topiaries and vines he cultivates. The neutral setting also allows him to find room for the spontaneous additions to his collections gleaned from regular trips to flea markets and antique shops.

The combination of whites with other cool colors, green and blue, has always been a favorite of the homeowner. The bedroom expresses his love for white and blue with striped linens layered on a white log bed; the bathroom shows his interest in white with green. With white walls and a summery linen shower curtain and sink skirt, the bathroom is the perfect setting for displaying the results of his green thumb — ivy creeps up the wall and side of the bathtub, replicating a scene from nature. The growing season may be limited, but with the residence this designer has shaped with naturals, he can enjoy the tranquillity of the outdoors year-round.

PASTELS

PASTELS ENLIVEN INTERIORS WITH INNOCENCE RATHER THAN BOLD DRAMA, LENDING ROOMS THE CHARACTERISTICS OF BRIGHT COLORS WITHOUT INSISTING ON THEIR FULL IMPACT: PINK MAY RADIATE EMOTION, BUT IT WILL NEVER DELIVER THE HIGH-PITCHED PASSION OF RED; POWDER BLUE WILL CONVEY RELAXATION, BUT NOT NAVY'S REGAL DEMEANOR. MELLOW BLENDS OF BRIGHT COLORS AND WHITE, PASTELS ARE BRIDGE TONES THAT CAN BALANCE AND HARMONIZE COLORS FROM BOTH ENDS OF THE SPECTRUM. WHITE MOLDINGS AND DOORS MARSHAL THE DIFFUSED TONES OF PASTELS, NUDGING THE COLOR FORWARD INTO THE ROOM. PASTEL WALLS CAN PICK UP ON THE COLORS OF THE MORE PROMINENT ACCESSORIES IN A ROOM, YET NEVER QUITE TURN THEM LOOSE — AS WHITE WALLS DO — OR COMPETE WITH THEM FOR ATTENTION — AS DEEPLY COLORED WALLS DO. PASTELS ARE PERFECT

partners for furniture and accents dressed either brightly or in white, and, in any given space, they tie together a wide variety of textures and patterns as well as colors. A muted chartreuse wall will make the visual transition from a red Oriental carpet to an off-white sofa seem less extreme; soft green walls will give a living room filled with white slipcovers greater depth. Pastels bring to mind the nuances of nature and so work well with furnishings that also speak of nature: flowered fabrics, beaded-board walls, wicker chairs, sisal mats. With their lighthearted personality, pastels also make rooms decorated with formal furnishings more welcoming. A dining room outfitted with mahogany furniture will feel more relaxed and congenial with pale walls. Pastels capture the heartwarming quality of warm temperatures, while at the same time adding a touch of coolness. By day, pastels broadcast their hints of color clearly without dominating a space. At night, when there is less light available to reflect off their white content, they look paler and more subdued. But pastels can always be counted on to enliven a room and gently add a casual flair.

Pastels harmonize light and dark colors. The sage green walls of a long living room (opposite) balance the warm tones of the coffee table and sisal rug with coolness and soften the glare of the white slipcovers. The green all but fades to white in the fireplace wall, reflecting the sensitivity of pastels to lighting conditions. At a sitting area at the opposite end of the room (above), the green walls are a gentle foil for primary-colored accent pillows.

Soft gray-green woodwork in a dining room (above) proves that pastels are an effective way to subtly highlight architectural features, such as window trim and wall paneling, and camouflage unsightly fixtures, such as a radiator. The pastel green connects the light cream walls to the deep Oriental carpet and the dark wood furniture and also creates a fluid connection between the room and the garden by echoing the foliage outdoors. Warm and lively, tan woodwork unifies a sitting room (opposite) by bridging the floor's dark brown hue and the sofa's rich background color with the white walls — any darker shade on the door or fireplace mantel would shrink the sense of space in the room and make it feel drab. A pale chartreuse wall (overleaf) is lively enough to look good with red and mellow enough to work well with white. It energizes the neutral furnishings in the living room with soft color and smooths the visual transition between them and the vivid hues of the Oriental carpet and wood pieces. Light green accessories introduce additional shades of green that help bring together the room's varied elements.

Pastel green trim in a dining room (left) emphasizes the orderliness of the room's structure, enhances its architectural interest, and strengthens its connection to the lush yard visible through a pair of French doors. The white paint on the walls in both the dining room and the adjacent sitting room (above) has been mixed with a hint of the trim color and thus fosters a sense of tranquillity. Blue print fabrics used in both spaces keep the rooms cool, while wood furniture and sisal rugs balance this coolness with warm browns and tans, and the effect is both soothing and refreshing. Decorating the two rooms with the exact same palette allows the eye to move easily from one space into the other and visually expands the size of the rooms.

Since their intensity is adaptable —
the paler a pastel, the more white has
been added; the more vibrant it is,
the less white has been added — pastels
work in public spaces and in rooms
where privacy is a consideration with
equal finesse. The pale yellow on the
walls of a foyer (top left) makes it feel
large and casts a warm and hospitable
glow. Red, which radiates even more
warmth than yellow and is more intense,
makes a cozy companion color on
a striped chair and rug. Salmon-toned
walls fill a dining room (bottom left)
with joy and warmth. Salmon is less
stimulating than orange, but almost as
enticing. Hot — but not searing —
color like this is great for a room that's
meant for eating and entertaining.

A bedroom can feel restful without being somber. A bright peach wall
with tan striped wallpaper (opposite
top) has a gentle way of perking up a
room where the furniture is sober in
tone. The lively bedspread with touches

of pale yellow, green, and peach —
colors that are repeated in the wallpaper
border — shows how a whole family
of pastels can work together to imbue
a room with livable charm.

Cool gray-green belongs on the
wall of a bedroom (bottom right)
where serenity is a top priority. This
subtle shade of green bridges the
gap between the bed's gunmetal gray
frame and the white bedspread and
beige accessories. Simple lace panels at
the windows diffuse the incoming
light and add to the serene and restful
character of the room.

In a living room (overleaf), pink
walls and a rose carpet evoke an atmosphere of sweet romance rather than
the sort of unbridled emotion that red
unleashes. The pastel walls help to
harmonize the casual furniture with the
more formal pieces. This room is more
heartwarming than festive, more subdued than dynamic — yet it is an upbeat
place in which to relax and entertain.

A bedroom (opposite) achieves a balance pleasing to the eye by placing a cool pastel, green, next to a warm one, pink. Mixing two colors that lie opposite each other on the color wheel, here pastel tones of red and green, and that have the same tonal value, the same amount of black or white in them, creates decorative harmony. The sweet shade of green lends serenity to the liveliness of the pink and reins in its exuberance. In another bedroom (above), the same pastel green, used on the walls, in the window treatments, and on the floor, presents another formula for decorating success — using equal amounts of a cool color and white in a room. Here, the application of color is executed with fabric as well as paint. Crisp white bed linens are a match for a wall painted pastel green; and a white canopy holds its own next to the window treatment it mirrors. The wall shelf and distressed finish on the drawers of the small bureau repeat the same soothing shade of green. Both colors, pastel green and white, work in concert to create a tranquil and relaxing room.

The owners of an 1886 Victorian house in Maine, set on a hilltop with a view of the Atlantic, renovated the interiors to brighten them and to forge a connection to the sky and the sea that is the setting for the house. A sky blue and white quilt and a paler blue ceiling (left) join a white bed and walls to create a serene and restful bedroom. In the bathroom (above), the pale seafoam green of the wall is echoed in the color of the rag rug. The cloud, sky, and sea theme gets full play in the home's living room (overleaf), where deeper tones of the same essentially cool palette suggest the natural scenery and casual architecture of the house's seaside location. In this room, a richly painted floor is an anchor for the pastel upholstery and helps produce a room that is filled with light and calm.

A HAVEN BELOW

Dark and gloomy, the dirt cellar below the kitchen addition of an 1846 Colonial cottage was the kind of space that was entered only by a gritting of the teeth and a determined focus on the task at hand — laundry.

Though its owner, an interior designer, managed to turn a blind eye to the blight for several years, she eventually decided to winterize her home for year-round use and, in the process, make her cellar more conducive to extended stays and multiple functions. As a child, she had loved playing in her English grandmother's basement, which, though a laundry room, had been decorated with chintz and china; the home-owner was now determined to create an attractive basement of her own that could accommodate family members and fill them with equally pleasant memories.

An advocate of using combinations of pale natural hues to create serene rooms, the designer felt no qualms about extending this brightening palette to a space normally filled with cinder block and murky gray tones. But she also wanted to incorporate a color that could add even more light and life to a room sealed off from views of the sky and trees — one that would be more vibrant than her preferred color scheme but one that would not be too adventurous or stray too far from the dove gray of an adjacent hallway.

To that end, she applied a cheerful celadon paint to beaded-board paneling, turning it into a room-expanding backdrop for herb plants and ivory, white, and beige accents — a sisal floor mat, a natural canvas sink skirt, a Shaker-style ironing board, a rack for air-drying linens, and a ceramic washbowl. She added French doors to block off the exterior stairway yet let in the light.

As a result of the designer's creative eye and handiwork, the cellar has become a soothing and cheerful sanctuary. With the addition of a dresser and youth bed, it also serves as a guest room for visiting nieces and nephews who cannot wait to go below. The cottage's bottom level is now an example of the power of cool pastels to nourish body, spirit — and family.

BEYOND THE PALE

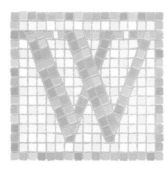

With just the right cast of colors and mix of accessories, any home — whether it's a large family house or a small cabin — can display casual country flair. Recognizing that pastels lend a friendly face to most anything they touch, the owner of a sweeping Greek Revival house selected a range of pale hues — sunny yellow, tan, and powder blue — as the backdrop for grand architectural details and both formal and casual furnishings. A white foyer composed of interesting woodwork sets the airy tone of the house at its entry. With its hint of yellow, a sunny color carried through the living room and dining room, the entry gives an indication of the comforting atmosphere that prevails throughout despite the house's stately structure.

In the living room, the yellow walls provide a contrast to the brilliant sapphire and ruby damask fabrics, lustrous round mahogany table, and gleaming hardwood floors. The formal room is mellowed further by the addition of a checkered rag rug and drapes of cotton ticking. In the dining room, the same shade of yellow on the walls softens the impact of the formal furniture yet enhances the inherent warmth of the woods. Pastel yellow is a good color choice for areas in which people come together because it imbues the rooms with a lighthearted cheer.

In the family room, tan — a pale version of brown — coats wainscoting, window trims, and moldings. The tan projects a warm, earthy feeling and holds its own against the more vibrantly colored country decorating accents — red gingham checks, plaid and floral textiles, and redware plates — with their bold charm. These colors help turn the room into a cozy center of activity. In the bedroom, the homeowner applied a cool pale blue to the walls and juxtaposed it with neutral linens and upholstery to create a tranquil retreat distinct in feeling from the more public rooms. All the pastels used in this home are perfectly suited to the functions of the rooms they appear in, and subtly shape both atmosphere and appearance.

The entry hall of a Greek Revival house features a built-in table, roomy closets, and two commanding round Doric columns all painted in bright white. The yellow border at ceiling level, echoed in a small window valance, foreshadows what is to come in the attached living room and in the rest of the house, where an array of pastels is put to work to fashion a relaxing country atmosphere amid stately furnishings and architecture.

Pastel yellow as it's used in the living room of a Greek Revival home (left), framed in cool white crown moldings, woodwork, and imposing fluted columns, is a rousing color. The yellow and white work together to set off the dark hardwood floors and jewel-toned damask upholstery and to highlight the casual drapes, made of cotton ticking.

In the dining room (above), the yellow walls and the gleaming brass light fixtures add a liveliness that softens the more reserved formal furniture. The same soft blue and white striped ticking of the living room's drapes has been used on the upholstered chairs and in the casual window treatment, lending the room a relaxed air.

In the family room (opposite), tan beaded-board wainscoting and distinctive window trim form a warm framework that plays up the beige and red floral, check, and plaid fabrics used in the seating, but does not overpower them. The tan trim and white walls allow the furniture to be the focal point of the room. The love seat with its red floral pillows, the overstuffed plaid armchairs, and the leather ottoman that's used as a coffee table make a cozy and invigorating conversation circle. The pastel blue in the master bedroom (above), a backdrop for an elegant sleigh bed dressed in antique white linens, generates the exact opposite atmosphere — cool tranquillity that is conducive to sleep. The creamy linen-colored chaise longue, rug, and window shades — made with buttons and buttonholes that are used to draw them back in an intriguing way — play against the pastel walls to create a pale and subdued version of a traditional blue and yellow color scheme.

I G H T S

YELLOW

A VASE OF SUNFLOWERS OR A BOWL OF LEMONS FILLS A KITCHEN WITH CHEER. A YELLOW QUILT ENERGIZES A BEDROOM WITH WARMTH AND COZINESS. NO MATTER WHAT SHADE OF YELLOW IS USED IN A ROOM — PALE CITRUS, RICH MUSTARD, OR BURNT OCHER — WHETHER IT ENTERS GINGERLY IN JUST A FEW SMALL ACCESSORIES OR BURSTS BOLDLY ONTO THE SCENE ON WALLS AND FURNITURE, IT IS IMPOSSIBLE TO IGNORE ITS GLOWING PRESENCE. YELLOW IS LIGHT WITH WARMTH AND CHEERFULNESS. YELLOW WALLS AND FABRICS IN A DINING ROOM OR LIVING ROOM PROMOTE THE CONGENIAL GATHERINGS THAT ARE THE FOCUS OF THESE SPACES. EVEN THE MOST FORMAL FURNITURE INVITES COMFORT AND RELAXATION WHEN UPHOLSTERED IN YELLOW OR ARRANGED AGAINST YELLOW WALLS. YELLOW PLACED IN A DIM ROOM OR ONE PACKED WITH WOOD FURNITURE MAKES IT FEEL WASHED IN

Brilliant yellow window trims and stair railings give a foyer (above) a welcoming personality. A harmonious blend of yellow tones simulating the antique blocks of a Tuscan villa (opposite) expands the horizons of a tight stairwell. A mural directs the eye outward and gives the sense that natural light is streaming in.

light — as if an entire wall of windows had been flung open. This makes it an excellent choice in historical homes, which are often dark and cramped. Mustard yellow was a frequently used color in Colonial times, and the use of yellow in older homes today enhances their old-world charm. Yellow is an ideal color for a hallway or entryway, too, because it conveys hospitality. Its high visibility also makes it an appropriate choice for areas and surfaces where personal safety is a concern. Yellow with touches of black, as on school buses and "yield" signs, has a graphic quality that makes people take notice. For all its extroverted exuberance, yellow also serves as a catalyst for serious pursuits, promoting intellectual activity as well as a rich

inner life — home offices and family rooms where activities range from games to homework to adult work can benefit from the mentally stimulating atmosphere that yellow provides. And yellow adds vitality to other colors: It makes hot hues such as red even more brilliant and brings cool colors such as blue and green to life, and is therefore a color that can restore balance to a decorating scheme. Almost every culture has a tradition of combining yellow and blue to both brighten and expand the sense of space in a room. Yellow and white also make a well-balanced pair: White becomes less glaring and cold next to yellow, and yellow appears less harsh alongside white. The two together make rooms feel warm, airy, and polished. Yellow, in fact, lets anything it touches shine.

Yellow on every surface — from walls and carpeting to baseboard and railings (opposite) — ensures that a house looks and feels sun-drenched, and in such an environment, wood and wicker can never look dull. Yellow plays up the many woven textures in the space and is a perfect balance for the muted and vivid hues. Kitchens are for congregating and cooking, and yellow strikes a positive note for each activity — even on cabinetry (left). The yellow walls in this kitchen pale by comparison to the yellow stain used on the cabinets and trims, but these small touches are enough to heat up the complexion of the room. The black wrought-iron hardware and chandelier lend a graphic quality to the yellow that is especially eye-catching. Using fabrics in addition to paint to create an all-yellow room (overleaf) greatly expands its visual interest and makes it appear less monochromatic than it really is.

Even yellow can go flat if there's no
visual relief in sight. In a living
room (opposite), the reverse sofa fabrics,
pillows, rug, and earthy pottery
layer in different shades of yellow as
well as a variety of textures and patterns that give the room added interest.
Gold, which is but yellow in a richer,
more luminous guise, is a natural
addition — here a trio of brass candle-
sticks brightens the table. In what
could have been a somber bedroom
(top right), a yellow nineteenth-century
Maryland quilt spread over the bed
offers a ray of light that's reflected in
the yellow paint on the built-in
cabinet. In a bedroom full of western
motifs (bottom right), the shapes
of plates hung on the yellow walls are
echoed in the quilt. Together they
brighten the dark woodsy surroundings.

You can mix and harmonize a wide variety of patterns in a room if they share a common palette. In this bedroom (left), yellow unifies a plaid dust ruffle, stylized botanical print duvet cover and pillow shams, and striped wallpaper and window shades. But yellow is not the only thing these accessories have in common; they are also casual patterns. These fabrics together with such lighthearted touches as fabric-covered lamp shades, a crocheted tablecloth on the night table, and a cotton rug soften the imposing formal furnishings. The pillows on the bed (above) are a cheerful mix of the fabrics used in the room tempered with solid yellow and white.

Blue and yellow together lend a lively rustic flavor to any room; they form a color scheme that lives happily in many cultures around the world. In a low-ceilinged living room (above), blue fabrics combine with yellow wainscoted walls and window trim to breathe fresh air into a room full of cozy clutter. A sitting room (opposite) shows that the marriage of yellow and blue cuts across boundaries of style and time — while this room has a modern bearing, it is still a bastion of casual comfort. The striped pillows, upholstered chairs, and leafy wallpaper border lace the yellow's punch with the serenity of blue. The key to this radiant space is a variety of shades of yellow and blue that match one another in tonal quality.

When yellow's warmth is not quite enough, a dash of red will increase the intensity — both are primaries with a passion. In a sitting room (above), a painted corner cabinet and prim sofa generate excitement against pale yellow walls and curtains. The striped rug harmonizes the colors used in the space at floor level where red is gripping but not overwhelming. Red doesn't have to be in the same room with yellow (opposite) to wield its decorative power, just in the same view. Bright yellow used on the staircase balusters in the entryway is framed by the red cabinetry in an adjacent kitchen in a way that charges up the yellow, boosting its decorative power. A hot color in one room, here the kitchen, that leads to a bright one in another, here the entry, helps ease the visual transition between the two spaces.

FRONT DOORS

N o other part of a facade delivers such potent messages about a home as the front door, and a house with a vivid front door is a house with street smarts. The front door provides an opportunity to link the outside of the house to the inside and offers clues to the decor. Because the door occupies only a small area of the front, it presents a chance to punctuate a pale house with bright color without disturbing its neutral look. Depending on the color chosen, a front door can exude warmth and hospitality or be more reserved. A saturated yellow door set into lemony clapboard makes no mistake about its meaning: This home is warm, upbeat, and inviting. On an all-wood house, a dark red door that turns mauve in the evening light is echoed inside in the foyer and stairwell. Like a blue door that makes a splashy entrance into a white interior, any front door coated in color can be the bright spot of the house and a hopeful hint of what awaits inside.

PASSING THROUGH A PALETTE

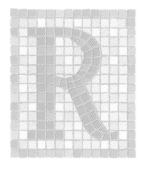enowned for his riveting blends of color on canvas, Impressionist painter Claude Monet applied his progressive understanding of hue to his own farmhouse in Giverny, France, painting each room a different color and providing a distinct visual experience from one room to the next. Inspired by the bold use of color in his Gallic home, these homeowners shaped an eating and food preparation suite — a dining room, pantry, and kitchen — that reinterprets Monet's palette. Passage through the suite provides an experience in the richness of color.

Sometimes three is a crowd, but the three colors used here — yellow, green, and blue — don't clamor for attention or crowd one another; applied to this suite of rooms, the colors create a cheerfulness that becomes intense calm as one moves through the space. Painted in rich yellow, the dining room and connecting passage set a warm tone that continues into the adjacent pantry and kitchen even as wall colors begin to cool down. The pantry, lined in deep green cabinets and wainscoted shelving units, features a slick blue and green tile backsplash. Appropriate to its central position, the pantry wears a color that is composed of the colors the other rooms sport — yellow and blue; and it displays them in a dramatic display of dishware.

The other rooms, too, weave in tones found elsewhere in the suite so that even as the spaces contrast, they harmonize with one another: The dining room features blue vines in the tile fireplace surround and blue stripes in the chair cushions, while the kitchen includes shades of cream and yellow in its plaid shades and tile backsplashes. A freestanding cabinet unit in the kitchen provides a view into the dining room, giving the sense of a high-noon sun piercing a cool blue sky.

This partition is more than a window onto the dining room; it is a window onto a classic color composition. Though it is French in inspiration, borrowed from one of the world's great painters, its true origin is in nature.

A yellow passageway (opposite) separates a dining room from a pantry whose brass drawer pulls echo the sunny color of the dining room. Based on Claude Monet's home in Giverny, the grand color scheme allows the eye to harmonize highly contrasting colors in the same way an Impressionist painting does. Blue and white checked fabric panels soften the vibrant green cabinetry in the pantry (overleaf). A wall of open shelving with a beaded-board back displays glazed pottery from France in colors that reflect the palette used throughout the cooking and entertaining suite.

The kitchen of the three-room suite revolves around blue, but also features small touches of cream, a toned-down version of the dining room's yellow. Five different patterns of blue and cream tile (above) give the cooking area a bold graphic quality that holds its own against the vibrancy of the painted cabinetry, walls, window frames, and ceiling beams: bold blue frames with pale blue interiors. The gleaming brass lighting fixture and faucets (right), the copper molds on the shelf above the range, and the array of copper cookware that hangs from a wall-mounted shelf enhance the warmth extended by the creamy wall tiles and the brown and russet tones in the vinyl floor and cherry work table. The kitchen, which is visible from the vivid green and blue pantry, is a beautifully balanced mix of cool and warm color.

A freestanding cabinet in the kitchen (above), which functions as a pass-through to the dining room and facilitates serving, epitomizes the character of the entertaining suite — saturated color and interior views. It shares the vivid blue colors of the kitchen cabinetry and brings the citrus yellow of the dining room into the kitchen to play off the creamy tile. The dining room's monochromatic color scheme (opposite), yellow walls, ceiling, china cabinet, and chairs, provides a dramatic contrast to the blues that prevail in the kitchen. But here, as in the adjoining rooms, small areas of color that dominate elsewhere in the suite help unify its three main areas: The chair pads and drapes contain blue stripes and the fireplace features three tile patterns that appear in the kitchen.

RED

RED IS BOLD AND BOISTEROUS. THERE IS NOTHING RESERVED ABOUT THE VERBAL DESCRIPTIONS IT INSPIRES, SUCH AS "SEEING RED" AND "RED HOT." RED CONNOTES EMOTION — ANGER, PASSION, AND RECKLESSNESS — AND SPEAKS OF AN UNINHIBITED LOVE OF LIFE. RED IN ANY ROOM STIRS UP FEELINGS, RAISES THE TEMPERATURE, QUICKENS THE PACE OF ALL THAT OCCURS AROUND IT, ENCOURAGES CREATIVITY — AND EVEN STIMULATES PLANT GROWTH! THOUGH IT NEVER RETREATS, RED IS MOST PRONOUNCED IN BRIGHT LIGHT; IT IS THE FIRST COLOR TO FADE IN DIM ILLUMINATION. A RED ROOM BY DAY PROVIDES A DIFFERENT EXPERIENCE FROM THE SAME ROOM BY NIGHT. BUT NO MATTER WHAT THE LIGHTING CONDITIONS AROUND IT, RED ENTICES, DRAWS ATTENTION, AND DOMINATES. THE COLOR OF MANY LUSCIOUS FRUITS, RED IS A ROUSING BACKDROP FOR ROOMS WHERE FOOD IS THE FOCUS.

If red's intensity is a scary proposition, consider mellowing it with white and adding it to a room in measured doses — on woodwork that outlines a historic country kitchen (above left), or on tucked-away spots, such as a banister and bay window frame in a stairwell (above right). In a dining room (opposite), white brightens and reins in a deep red to encourage warm gatherings and great meals.

No other color creates a more festive or celebratory mood — red is the preferred color of Chinese brides, Latin dancers, and Spanish bullfighters. Weathered and worn historical structures seem to come back to life once red is introduced into the room. Rich in tone, red implies abundance and is a lively prescription for luxury. Gold accessories, such as gilded mirrors, therefore look wonderful with it. Red has long been associated with Oriental carpets and Victorian shawls and so welcomes many different sensibilities into a country interior; it is a color that lets a wide range of fabrics and wallpapers live well together. White touches placed alongside red subdue its drama and enhance its inherent charm; a kitchen or dining room where red appears in a dainty wallpaper print or a striped fabric is a room that conveys friendliness. That is why, in addition to the sense of luxe it imparts, red can be counted on to be as down-home and all-American as apple pie. It is a color with true staying power and its allure lies in the warmth it radiates.

A red and white printed wallpaper perks up a dining room full of old country furniture (above). An Oriental carpet and window swag carry red's spunky rhythm into an adjacent living room, creating a sense of friendly and familiar comfort. Red cookware and small appliances (opposite) amplify the cheerful country feeling generated by a red and white checked wallpaper on a kitchen backsplash. Cozy charm is not the only mood country does well (overleaf). This room proves that rustic design can be passionate as well. With a coat of high-gloss red, the walls all but vibrate. The seating, curtains, and fireplace surround provide cool counterpoints, yet this is hardly a place to sink back and relax; it's a feisty spot to rejoice in and celebrate.

A stove is not the only way to heat up a kitchen. An oil-base red paint, thinned down, that allows the natural wood grain pattern on birch kitchen cabinetry to show through does the job as well (opposite). Lovely floral tiles from Portugal and a Victorian maple countertop add contrasts in texture to the cabinets. The scientific principal that heat rises makes a compelling decorative concept in this room: Cover a mellow wood floor with soft rag rugs and work up to the heat of the pulsating red cabinets. In a historical room where the walls are weathered and worn planks (above), vibrant red upholstery offers a rejuvenating jolt. When the ceiling is low, concentrating color near the floor helps open up the room.

This is a living room (left and above) that goes to extremes by defying decorating guidelines. Red on walls, windows, a mantel, and furniture creates a room that is hot-blooded, rich, and almost over the top; but the wide range of patterns lives well in this small space because of the red they have in common. The furnishings seem to invite langour, but the explosion of pattern and color makes sure that the down time will never be dull. Only curtains in green, red's cool complement, provide a restful spot for the eye to land. In another all-red living room (overleaf), a different mix of fabrics — a boldly patterned cloth tossed over the coffee table, a rich paisley swath on a sofa, and drapes made of antique Spanish brocade — prove that red need be the only constant in a room. The deep red walls respond well to gold; they look elegant with a lineup of gilded frames that contribute to the room's layered sense of luxe.

ORANGE

Warm and earthy, orange hints at its own origins — red and yellow — and the sunbaked clays that sport its tone in nature. It combines yellow's good cheer and red's spirited stance, but leaves behind some of red's hot emotions. Mixed with white, orange becomes peach or salmon, both pleasing colors for rooms because they have red's warmth without its heat and, when reflected on the skin, cast a cheerful and flattering glow. Peach walls outlined in a more emphatic orange pro-duce an invigorating room that may spur more creativity than rest. In a living room, black accents, such as those in a richly patterned carpet, provide a refreshing contrast to deep peach. And because peach has a natural affinity for earth colors, it warmly embraces a range of browns from wood tones to russet. Orange is not for everyone — especially in its pure form, which can appear harsh. But carefully placed and balanced with white or black, orange fills a room with livable charm.

B L U E

Blue, the color of devotion, contemplation, and constancy, gives anything it dresses an added sense of dimension. In rooms, it raises the ceiling and pushes back the walls to forge an expansiveness that no other color can rival. As the phrase "true blue" implies, blue has always been associated with loyalty and reliability. It grounds rooms in tradition and defies trendiness even when it appears in contemporary furnishings and architecture. Decorating with blue is therefore less about taking chances than about playing it safe. Blue can be applied in any number of combinations and shades — from powder blue and cornflower blue to sapphire and navy — through layers of patterned fabrics and paint on trims and walls. When it's deep and dark, it lends a room a regal stature and a serious atmosphere; when it's light and airy, it envelops a space in simplicity

and sweetness. Blue plays a key role in many classic color schemes. Mix it with one long-standing partner, yellow, and it creates a palette familiar the world over, from the cold regions of Scandinavia to the warm zones of southern France. Pair it with white as in a gingham fabric or flow-blue china and it is both calming and lively at the same time, elegant but also friendly. Add some gray to blue and it becomes a color with a history, one that was used in Colonial homes on woodwork and utilitarian accessories and one that makes the most of light, enhancing the brightness of a room while never shedding its innate dignity. Juxtapose it with green and it becomes nature's own recipe for serenity. It is precisely this harmonious quality that makes blue appropriate for any room in the house. It is a favorite shade for bedrooms because it exudes comfort and ease; it makes an excellent color for a study because it fuels contemplation, deliberation, and accomplishment. Kitchens look especially dapper in blue; blue cabinets shape a pleasing backdrop for vibrant fruits and vegetables. Blue in any room fosters a feeling of balance and tranquillity.

Dark blue soaks up light. Framing it in white allows a room to benefit from blue's tranquillity without allowing it to dim the light. In a sitting room (opposite), white window trim brightens and mellows the surroundings. In the living room of an eighteenth-century home (above), dark blue on the woodwork suits the heft and weight of history, but gleaming white walls prevent the room from feeling dark or frozen in time. In a family room (overleaf), blues in many tints and shades create a calm and casual sanctuary.

The owner of a contemporary house in Connecticut gave the kitchen (left) a traditional character by adding barn-style posts and beams and Shaker-style cabinets. The distressed finish and maple pulls on the dark blue cabinets relieve the feeling of density so much dark blue could engender. Golden maple countertops and a beaded light shade contribute an orangy glow that complements the blue. The homeowner's collection of miniature chairs, including ladder-back chairs (above), that rest atop the cabinets and hang from forged-iron hooks spread small dots of rich color around the room, directing the eyes upward. In a historic kitchen in an 1825 home in upstate New York (overleaf), Shaker-style cabinets painted deep Prussian blue lend depth to the spare styling, while white backsplashes and appliances add a modern crispness. Vibrant fruits and vegetables look spectacular against this sedate but efficient backdrop.

Blue and white, one of the freshest color combinations and one that's easy to live with, always enlivens a room. The stone and wood structure of a living room (opposite top) is somber, but blue and white fabric pillows piled onto white sofas are a perfect antidote to the feeling of enclosure. Quilts draped over balcony railings and a patterned rug (top right) expand the blue and white theme up to the ceiling and down to the floor. In a formal bedroom and sitting room (opposite bottom), serious wood furnishings that could look stuffy instead exude friendliness because they're dressed with blue and white linens and surrounded by matching blue and white wallpaper. In this cool setting shaped with a variety of shades of blue ranging from lavender to navy (bottom right), the wood provides welcome spots of warmth.

The powder blue on the fireplace wall of a bedroom (above left), uninterrupted by pattern, expands the sense of space while drawing attention to the denser blue in the quilt. The intriguing pattern on the bed receives its due by not having to compete with a brighter color. The overall effect of this compilation of blues is tame and restorative, and appropriate for a bedroom. A view from a dressing room into a bedroom (above right) juxtaposes two different shades of blue, which propel the eye from one space into the other. The wallpaper in the dressing area, sprinkled with green flowers, dominates the view with a vibration set up by the blue and green combination. The light blue ceiling and quilt on the bed beyond have a calming effect that helps distinguish this space in which sleep occurs from the adjacent one in which activity is emphasized. In a Victorian-style bedroom (opposite), where dark woods, imposing furniture, and rich reds pose a challenge to a restful atmosphere, a light blue floral wallpaper serves as a refreshing background that tones down the formality and breathes new life into the room.

Matching a wall color to a dominant
accent or piece of furniture in a
room forms a powerful bond between
architecture and decor that strengthens
the sense of harmony in a space.
When that color is blue, the result is
pure comfort. In a dining room
(top left), the classic combination of
white and blue in china inspires a
decorating scheme composed of the
same colors around a wood table
and hutch. In a kitchen (bottom left),
a wall painted a sky blue and a tabletop in the same color form strong
counterpoints to dark cabinets that
would produce a gloomy space without
the expansive presence of blue. Though
this living room (opposite) is part of
a vintage log cabin, its style is decidedly
formal, and a blue settee in satiny
damask combines with a blue wall to
render it regal. Though blue is not
known for commanding center stage,
by providing respite from the heat of
several shades of red, the settee becomes
the true focal point of the room.

A cozy family room (left) provides a lesson in how to make a structural element the center of attention: Surround it with its complementary color. With its cool blue-green frame, the ruddy brick fireplace all but leaps off the wall. Arched bookshelves painted a butter yellow and a mustard yellow ottoman serve as secondary focal points that help create a sense of balance in the room. In a kitchen (above), a bank of cabinets gains interest by having its doors and drawer panels painted a saturated blue-green that pops out from a baby blue background. The palette is reversed on the top level, where the baby blue predominates and serves to accentuate the contents of the cabinet rather than the cabinet itself. The interplay of dark and light blues sets up a playful visual rhythm in the space.

PURPLE

Purple, we're told, is the color we're not supposed to use to decorate our homes. Its reputation for being difficult is not unfounded; it is a mix of blue and red — two colors whose placement at opposite ends of the spectrum make it hard to focus on. Yet purple can be used successfully in either a pale or rich tone and lends a space the best of both colors that compose it: red's warmth and blue's clarity. Historically a color associated with royalty, purple conveys both grandeur and sensitivity and makes a surface unique and special. The lighter the version of purple used, the easier it is to use in a decorating scheme. Lavender on a single wall adds a glimmer of excitement to a restful blue and white composition without dispelling a sense of calm. A deeper tone of purple exudes pure fun and joy. Used on a limited expanse and paired with white, a natural partner, it creates an eye-catching combination that adds liveliness to a space without overwhelming it.

GREEN

FROM THE GRAY-GREEN OF A FERN TO THE EMERALD GREEN OF A CASCADING VINE TO THE CITRUS GREEN OF A GRANNY SMITH APPLE, NATURE DISPLAYS A BROAD RANGE OF VERDANT TONES. TO BRING THEM INSIDE IS TO CREATE A SENSE OF THE OUTDOORS IN INTERIORS; IN CLIMATES WHERE GROWING SEASONS ARE SHORT, ROOMS FILLED WITH GREEN HAVE THE JOYFUL FEELING OF SPRINGTIME. GREEN WALLS AND ACCESSORIES IN SUNROOMS, PORCHES, AND OTHER SPACES WITH WINDOWS AND GLASS-PANED DOORS CREATE A SMOOTH VISUAL FLOW BETWEEN THE INDOOR AND OUTDOOR SPACE. IN NATURE, DEEP SHADES OF GREEN ALMOST ALWAYS OVERLAP MORE MELLOW ONES, BUT NO MATTER HOW VARIED THE GREENS IN A GIVEN SETTING ARE, THEY ACCOM-MODATE ONE ANOTHER AND CREATE A SENSE OF HARMONY. A WIDE RANGE OF GREEN TONES CAN BE USED SUCCESSFULLY INDOORS, TOO.

Sunlight streaming into a room filled with green accessories against white walls (above) makes it feel like a gardener's Eden — a refreshing space that transcends the limits imposed by windows and doors. White walls and furniture seem to evaporate (opposite) when framed by deep green baseboards and chair rails, allowing the framed botanical prints to dominate the space.

Far from the vanguard, green appears normal and conventional. The hunter green carpeting combined with dark wood furnishings and fixtures often found in banking and law offices shows what green projects: trust, order, and repose. Green offers a feeling of serenity as well as clarity and has been shown to reduce tension in the body and mind. This calming influence is the reason for the frequent use of green in public buildings, such as hospitals and schools, where a restful and rejuvenating environment is important. At home, too, green in bedrooms and studies promotes rest and contemplation and turns these spaces into refuges from hectic schedules. But even as it soothes, green makes its presence known. Green on unsung spaces like stairwells and hallways calls attention to their interesting features without lending them more importance than the rooms they connect. Green used around white or muted woods will step forward just as it does in nature. The combination of wood

and green is an ideal blend of warmth and coolness that works well in a sitting room or kitchen, where nurturing backgrounds are desired. Though green is relied upon for the constancy it conveys, if it is linked to a more vibrant hue it becomes more flexible and picks up the attributes of the colors it is around. Green and red, opposites on the color wheel and a combination popular in folk art, projects a bold charm. Green and white — or any of its variations, such as olive green and cream — is a thoroughly country combination because it re-creates the sense of balance found in nature. When mixed with yellow, green fills up with light; limes and acid greens create settings that are more challenging than consoling. Blue fills green with a lively, expansive quality and boosts its cooling touch. Green is decorating's security blanket; its greatness lies in the fact that it can ground a house in color and link it to its exterior setting.

An architecturally interesting stairwell (opposite), painted olive green, makes a welcoming entry. An antique writing desk finished with a reddish stain that echoes the color of the graceful handcrafted cherry balusters is the perfect complement for the green woodwork. A kitchen with gray-green cabinets (above) has cream walls and a yellow floor, colors no less earthy, as warm foils for the cool green.

A formula for plush and serious-minded surroundings like law offices, banks, and private clubs — dark green and dark wood — always looks dapper. The dark green living room walls (above) evoke the luxurious leathers found in such formal settings, but light wood trims, white uphol-stery, and uncurtained windows eliminate the old-world feeling by keeping things bright and open. Like an overgrown garden, all-green cabinets in a kitchen (opposite) could feel too closed in, but when they are placed against the light wood logs, the room gains a sense of balance. The vinyl floor's red diamond, bordered in cooler colors, gives the room a spirited core derived from the wisdom of Amish quilt makers: Every cool spot benefits from the touch of a warm hand. When green kitchen cabinets have a weathered finish (overleaf), a play of texture against texture — wood against stone — seems appropriate. The kitchen's original stone floor and the intricate tortoiseshell finish on the countertops complement the green cabinets because both palette and materials are taken from nature.

White empowers green, adding light to its cool darkness. In a country bedroom (opposite), white preserves an open feeling, allowing the green wall to take center stage and to give the room a feeling of rest and relaxation. Against the contrasting green backdrop, the reddish brown armoire projects warmth. In two historical bathrooms, white and green compose a recipe for Shaker-style repose. In one (top right), a Shaker peg strip and backsplash moldings in gray-green create order around a sink. In the other (bottom right), bright white walls reflect light around a dark green bath-tub enclosure, imparting a refreshing look to the bathroom. When green brings the weight of history to bear on a room — as in a living room painted in classic Federal green (overleaf), bright white is uplifting, softening the prim-and-proper bearing of the room and grounding it firmly in the present.

Green is composed of blue and yellow, and the more yellow in the green, the more cheerful it is. Add yet more yellow and the green becomes almost animated. In a gardener's cottage (top left), a somber stone fireplace is brightened by sunlight streaming through the windows and warmed by the yellow-green walls. In a bedroom (bottom left), lime-green walls anchored by deep green moldings create a room that is not merely relaxing but revitalizing. The simple wood bed echoes the architecturally clean lines of the room, making it a restful retreat. The acid green walls of a dining room (opposite), set off by hunter green window trim, spice up the neutral wood and rustic woven textures that accessorize the room. A cone-shaped chair in the corner adds a theatrical note to a decidedly upbeat room.

MIXING IT UP

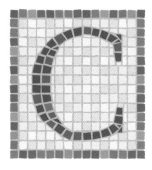

Choosing even one color for a room can be difficult, but choosing a combination of bold colors can be positively agonizing. It is far easier to evaluate a color scheme once the colors are in place than when they are merely swatches or paint chips in hand. Fortunately, trial and error is not the only method for assuring success. One effective way to choose colors that will work well together in a space is to let the cherished objects that will fill it be the guide. The architecture of a period home can also serve as a guidepost for using historically authentic colors or reinterpretations that are in keeping with contemporary tastes.

The owner of an 1890 Victorian home, a textile designer, sought color inspiration for a kitchen update in her exuberant collections. She chose a mix of high-gloss yellow, red, and baby blue on the cabinets that echoes the vibrant hues of the Fiesta ware bowls and other treasured collectibles. This textile designer's love of vintage fabrics, which she both collects and sells, prompted her to introduce additional color with a cheery 1940s tablecloth.

A storyteller and folk art collector also allowed her profession and collections to influence the decor of her childhood home. She furnished the dining room with a painted Tyrolean bureau, appliqué quilt, and Mexican chairs, all in bright colors. Her choice of soothing green for the walls and brilliant red for the window trims plays up the cheerful, primitive character of these furnishings.

To layer a similarly vibrant quality into the keeping room of a newly built house full of neutral woods, its owner reinterpreted a traditional Colonial palette. Investigation has proven that these historical colors are much more vivid than was previously thought, but the homeowner's particularly vital rendition of them is wonderfully suited to the contemporary setting. Letting beloved objects and classic palettes determine colors can make a bright and cheery scheme the right choice.

The textile designer owner of this kitchen (opposite) felt instinctively that bright colors can live as well together on kitchen cabinets as they do on a swath of fabric. She based the cabinetry's color scheme on colors found in the collection of ceramic ware that surround them — Fiesta ware bowls, 1930s Japanese majolica biscuit jars, and a grouping of clown cookie jars. The shiny yellow, red, and blue of the cabinets is echoed at floor level in a stenciled floorcloth with the graphic flair of a Mondrian painting.

A professional storyteller with an
appreciation for the narrative power
of folk art updated her childhood
home — a 1908 Arts and Crafts shingle-
style house in San Francisco — with
colors derived from a collection of
primitive and cheerful folk art pieces
that include a painted Tyrolean
bureau (left). The red window trims and
the calming green on the walls play
off the colors of the 1925 floral appliqué
quilt that hangs on the wall and
are repeated in the Mexican chairs that
surround the French country table.
These bold colors create an atmosphere
that is both innocent and playful.

In a newly constructed keeping
room outfitted with light woods
(overleaf), a classic Colonial color
scheme — determined by architectural
historians to be quite rich — was
tweaked by the homeowner to be yet
bolder. These neo-American color
interpretations, a vibrant blue-green
paint on the wainscoting above
the fireplace and yellow and white
teacup and coin dot fabrics on
the chairs and settees, inject a sense
of life into the neutral setting.

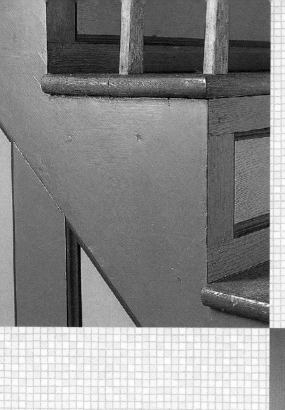
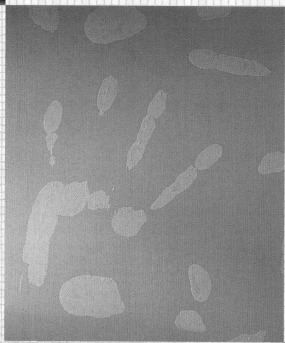
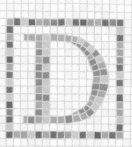

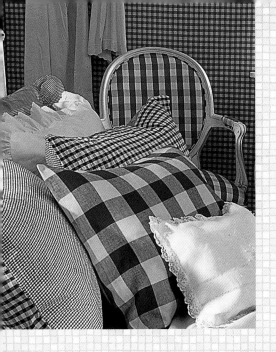

ESIGN

PAINT

No feature in home design is as easy to use and as inexpensive as paint. Through its deft application, a room can be brought to life with the richness and panache of color. Architecture becomes more friendly, and each surface of a room becomes an opportunity to draw the eye with texture, pattern, and light. Every wall is imbued with potential — of looking taller, deeper, farther away or closer in. Depending on the colors used, windows, mantels, moldings, and doors stand out in bold relief or all but disappear, altering the mood of a space and changing the perception of its size. A fresh coat of paint can make a time-worn room or piece of furniture step into the present, refreshed and ready for the demands of today, or lend a contemporary space the captivating signs of age. Paint

allows the possibility of creating a balance between warm and cool hues in a room and of creating rhythm and depth by alternating light and dark tones. The array of age-old country techniques for covering surfaces, walls, beams, and floors with paint to enhance the visual interest of a room is vast — from stenciling to dragging, ragging, sponging, combing, stippling, and graining. Weathered and worn furnishings found at garage sales, flea markets, and antiques shops can be resuscitated as well. A decorative mural painted on a living room or hallway wall opens up a room to the outside and provides new dimensions to explore. All these techniques evoke other eras, climates, and locales and shape marvelous backdrops for antiques and collectibles. Yet the sense of depth and artistry they contribute is far greater than the effort required to achieve their special effects. Whether paint is mixed by hand or chosen from the large collections offered by major companies or from smaller companies that use historically accurate pigments, paint provides a way to emblazon rooms with a country personality as well as a distinct brand of creativity.

In a dining room (opposite) with the warmth and time-faded character of a Mediterranean villa, a blue floor adds depth to the room and balances the warm peach walls. Here, a natural sponge, moistened with water and then soaked in glaze, was pressed over the base of peach paint to produce subtle variations of color. A boy's bedroom (above) has walls rag-painted in light blue. To achieve the softly mottled effect, the paint was applied with a roller, then rubbed with a cloth.

Murals are real eye-openers in a room, setting the walls and furnishings within imaginary landscapes. A high level of artistic skill is not needed to paint a primitive mural; many historical country homes featured walls with simple designs executed by itinerant, untutored artists. A mural depicting a grove of tall trees in a softly rolling landscape suffuses a bedroom (above) with a nourishing sense of the outdoors no matter what the season. The greens in the mural supply a cool foil to the red window swags and bed quilt. In a dining area (opposite), a nautical mural, a theatrical touch that lifts the spirits just as the soft blue tones relax them, transports the room to distant lands and times. In the process, the walls lose their sense of confinement.

While a pair of red doors adds exuberance to an old country kitchen (opposite), a stenciled quilt pattern in a complementary color, a refreshing sage green, offers the intrigue of pattern. Stencils that are ready to use are available in crafts stores, or patterns can be copied from books at a library. A checkerboard pattern (top right), created by stamping with a small sponge, traces the room's molding. It is an effective way to lend delicacy and an upward push to a room. The checkerboard pattern is simple to make and easy to work with. Both it and the sage green stencil create a lively look with only one color of paint. A more intricate botanical stencil design with swags and tassels (bottom right) works its way around a corner shelving unit, playing off the displayed china and drawing attention to its delightful designs.

Built-in shelving units for displaying
photographs, collections, and
books enrich any room. Painting the
wall that backs the shelves in a color
that contrasts with the walls that
surround them adds a certain vitality.
Dark blue gives added depth to the
shell portion of an arched niche
(above) while a bright red inside accentuates the china display. In a living
room (right), a crimson much darker
than the yellow walls charges up
the shelf units with emotional intensity
and directs attention to them.

Doors can be made daring with
paint, not only in rooms but also in
furniture. A stately display cabinet
(opposite) gains a spry attitude with a
painterly treatment on its doors.
The swirling blue-green color echoes
the wood grain and forges a connection between the cabinet and the
collectibles displayed inside.

By evoking bygone times when
expert craftsmanship was a fact of
everyday life, paneled doors add historical flavor to any room. Panels painted
differently from their frames sport
a geometric look. Green panels surrounded by reddish frames (top right)
reflect the fascination of complementary colors juxtaposed in a small
area; yellow interiors electrify their
dark wood trims (bottom right) and
duplicate the early-nineteenth-century
treatment, uncovered beneath thirty-
two coats of paint.

Wood can look rich and, as a natural material, always evokes nature's gifts. But a room filled with brown wood furniture runs the risk of looking somber and lifeless. Painted wood pieces can remedy that. A dining area (left) boasts a range of riveting country colors — bright yellow chairs enliven three cabinets painted in different shades of blue and green. Although the cabinets are large and imposing, their color makes them fun and friendly, and through them the room gains a down-home atmosphere. The green cabinet's distressed finish demonstrates the magic of wood that sports a hint of color—it implies an interesting history and the touch of human hands. The round dining table (above) also combines wood tones and paint, proving that a footing of color adds a lighthearted spirit to a room.

A floor painted in a checkerboard pattern can anchor a room in color and lend it bold graphic appeal without the need for many accessories or colored walls, especially in a space with very little wall area. In a sunroom punctuated by windows (opposite), white wicker furniture with muted striped pillows sustains the light and airy atmosphere of the room, while contrasting diamonds in the floor provide some punch. The green in the pillows and floor links the space to the outside. Similarly, a living room framed in floor-to-ceiling windows (top right) gets a calming lift from a blue and white floor that delivers panache without diverting attention from the winning views outside. In a bedroom with short side walls under a sharply sloping ceiling (bottom right), a pale olive and white checkerboard floor provides a decorative underpinning that adds depth at ground level and makes the space seem less cramped than it actually is; a carpet would only fill the space more.

In a room where an area rug runs the risk of getting soiled or wet, such as a kitchen, mud room, or porch, a painted rug adds pizzazz to the floor. While not strictly speaking a trompe l'oeil image — a French term that means fool-the-eye — which is an exact reproduction of a scene or item that can be mistaken for the real thing, a painted rug that uses stencils or free-hand patterns, relying on photographs or a real rug for inspiration, adds primitive charm to a room. A kitchen (above) boasts a fringed design composed of a variety of traditional country stencil patterns. Because of its layers of varnish, it can handle any spill. A small hand-painted throw (opposite) can withstand traffic and moisture and adds a spot of exuberance to an overlooked area.

A PLAYFUL SPIRIT

It's a challenge for any homeowner to create a kitchen that is both functional and beautiful. This serious work space that is also the all-purpose gathering room often runs to extremes, looking either sleek and clinical or overdecorated and barely serviceable. To find a decorative middle ground takes careful planning and ingenuity. But to give a kitchen a personal imprint takes even more than reflection and vision; it takes boldness. The creators of this kitchen in an early-nineteenth-century farmhouse, a cabinet designer and a trompe l'oeil artist, sought inspiration in the homeowners' six children and drew on childlike daring, filling the space with exaggerated forms and energetic free-flowing designs that recall the age of innocence. First they painted the kitchen in various shades of yellow, a long-standing country kitchen favorite, to lend it a cheerful, lighthearted appeal. And then, with every surface beaming and bright, the design team layered on a spontaneous sense of whimsy with moldings — in sawtooth shapes below the upper cabinets and in large scallop profiles above both the upper and lower tiers. These moldings, sponge-painted in a pale blue pattern that echoes the granite countertop's mottled appearance, transform the solid birch and poplar cabinet doors into lively surfaces that warrant more than a second look. Squiggly combed lines painted in a deeper shade of yellow crawl up and across each door, adding a playful sense of rhythm. Sporadically placed carved lines and dots enhance the buoyant impact. Not waiting for the kitchen to be marked by the telltale signs of the lives led within it, the designers layered some "art" of their own onto the deep yellow panels of the door — interpretations of children's handprints, reminders of the sort kids leave on every door they pass through. Flanked by wavy lines, the handprints on the door panels, along with the other paint treatments in this kitchen, add up to a formula for injecting exuberance, energy, and humor into a room that revolves around a single color.

WALLS OF WONDER

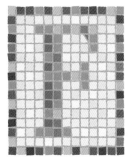

For the homeowner, a white wall is like an artist's blank canvas — a proverbial clean slate that begs for imagery or special textures and patterns that can give expression to personal interests and creative impulses and layer in beauty. One of the most dramatic and affordable ways to enhance walls and the spaces they enclose is to give them a decorative paint treatment. Though such a treatment affects the surface, the beauty it contributes is more than skin-deep. When different paint techniques are applied in combination with one another, the effect can be utterly fascinating — one which the eye will go back to again and again, tracing and exploring its intricacies in various areas of the room. Because paint finishes are executed by hand, no two areas ever look exactly the same, and it is this visual variety that accounts in large measure for the finishes' allure.

The owner of a 1750 farmhouse decided to apply a decorative paint finish to the kitchen walls to add not only color but imagery as well. Decorative artists hired by the homeowner painted the walls yellow and then sponge-painted in an earthy cinnamon around foliage picked from the house's grounds. The leaves served as templates that blocked out the paint as it was dabbed on with a sponge, leaving their forms behind as empty spaces surrounded by a dense but subtle pattern of dots.

Another homeowner opted to rejuvenate an attic study by rag-painting the walls and eaves in a stunning green-blue color that adds depth to the surface and presents a beautiful backdrop for an array of country collectibles.

While some find decorative power in elaborate paint treatments, others find it in the patchy, worn look of plaster walls left unpainted. These imperfect surfaces broadcast a rich sense of history and serve as interesting textured foils for formal furnishings. Whether one uses paint or not, these houses all support the notion that no home is finished until its walls have been finished.

A freewheeling pattern on a kitchen wall (opposite) created by sponge-painting over leaves and ferns provides a fitting naturalistic setting for a bronze bird nest sculpture and an urn filled with dried flowers that sit on an antique apothecary chest.

In an attic study (overleaf), cozily packed with wood tones and country collectibles, rag-painted walls supply beautiful color and pattern. The texture and age given these walls by rolling a twisted cloth dipped in a contrasting color of paint over a base coat add to its appeal. Though the walls slope in, the refreshing paint treatment keeps the eye moving and chases away any cramped feeling.

An avid collector brought a Federal-era row house back to life by outfitting it with spectacular examples of period furniture and accessories. While the plaster walls in the family parlor (left) have been patched, they have not been painted. Like the room's uncurtained windows and unfinished floor, the walls' stripped-down appearance reveals the glorious history of the room and provides an ideal backdrop for the rich early-nineteenth-century furnishings such as a rare marble-top center table, French lighting fixture, and bold blue and yellow Baltimore sofa with tasseled cushions and bolsters. The aged look of the walls highlights the perfection of a Wedgwood black basalt urn (above) that rests atop the parlor's mantel. A late-eighteenth-century oil painting in an elaborate gilded frame seems more grand against a wall where texture is more dominant than color.

HISTORIC PAINT

When the new owner took on the renovation of an 1825 tavern to make it into a home for his family, he restored much of its original flair by adding historically inspired color to both the interior and the exterior. He and two colleagues created the color with natural pigments following age-old recipes. Shiny, saturated, and placed in startling juxtapositions, the color choices play up the architectural strengths of the new home.

From the layers of paint that coat their exteriors and the pilasters that support them to the colors chosen for individual rooms, houses are documents of both their times and the personal tastes of the people who live in them. To discover and give homage to a house's roots, paint can be peeled back to bare its true colors, or, following this homeowner's lead, the color traditions of its architectural style can be explored and applied to the house.

Color trends change over the years, and virtually every style of house — from bungalow to English cottage to Dutch Colonial — is characterized by many different color combinations over the length of its life. To trace a house's trail of color, layers of paint can be chipped off in various places and the preferred combinations can be matched to colors in the historical color collections of major paint companies (found in paint supply stores). Or a professional color consultant — an expert in uncovering and analyzing original paint schemes — can determine colors that can then be chosen from the historical paints formulated with traditional pigments that are now available. To test color choices before painting an entire room or the whole house, dab them onto small areas and live with them in daylight and at night to see their changing looks.

While, generally speaking, a house's body color is more mellow than its trim color, historical colors were often far brighter than those in fashion today. The daring combinations based on period exteriors can be used inside as well, extending the excitement and richness to every room. House colors do not have to be historically accurate to make the most of a home, but taking cues from the past may fill it with depth.

FABRIC

FABRIC SOFTENS ARCHITECTURE AND EVOKES COMFORT AND CONTENT-MENT WITH ITS COLORS, GRAPHICS, TEXTURES, AND GENTLE FOLDS. SUPPLE SWATHS OF CLOTH POSSESS A DELICACY THAT ENVELOPS ANY SPACE IN BEAUTY AND WARMTH. WHEN LACE CURTAINS BILLOW AT A WINDOW, LIGHT AND AIR MAKE THEIR PRESENCE FELT INSIDE. A QUILT HUNG ON A WALL OR SPREAD OVER A BED IMMEDIATELY CONVEYS THE CREATIVE TOUCH OF THE HUMAN HAND AND A SENSE OF ROOTEDNESS. AND A ROW OF PLUMP PILLOWS ON A SOFA OR BANQUETTE EXTENDS AN INSTANT INVITATION TO SIT BACK AND RELAX. UPHOLSTERY, WHETHER POLISHED AND SUMPTUOUS OR NUBBY AND COARSE, TAMES A ROOM AND CAN ALSO FILL ITS VISUAL VOIDS WITH PATTERN. GINGHAM'S CHECKS BROADCAST A CASUAL AND FRIENDLY ATMOSPHERE; EMBROIDERED WORKS AND ANTIQUE LINENS ARE NOSTALGIC TOUCHES THAT LINK A ROOM

to a legacy of rapidly disappearing craftsmanship. Floral fabrics turn interior spaces into perenially blooming gardens. Fabric patterns are far more forgiving of one another than they are generally given credit for, and can be readily combined if they share common or compatible ingredients, such as color. Red stripes, for example, harmonize beautifully with yellow and white checks, since both incorporate straight lines and a good measure of warmth. Several patterns and colors layered over one another are seductive to the eye and bring depth and richness to the room. The more patterns used in a space, the fuller and denser it feels; a spare use of pattern conveys an open feeling. Perhaps the best feature of fabric, though, is its flexibility. It allows rooms to be quick-change artists: Throws, slipcovers, and pillows can alter the character of a room, adapting it with a new color to another season or point of view. A warmly colored fabric will direct attention to the spot in which it appears; but shift its placement and the room will gain an entirely new focus. That is the special character of fabric: Even a small touch — a seat cushion, a valance — supplies a rich core of color that can grip the eye in unexpected ways.

Color and pattern are powerful tools that when used effectively can shape the look and feel of a room. In a family room (opposite), checked pillows work well with a toile-like wallpaper and sofa fabric because of a shared palette. Lining the printed drapes with checked fabric enriches the play of design. A white-walled bedroom (above) gets its character from a layering of red and white botanical and plaid fabrics. Red and white quilted pillows (overleaf) — bold complements to the green sofa and drapes — show the lively effect of opposite colors in a neutral room.

A fabric color that is warmer, bolder, or deeper in tone than the walls surrounding it has a way of taking over a room. The long, puddled red curtains in a bedroom (above) not only accentuate the height of the room and create a dramatic backdrop for the bed but also make it a true focal point. The red coverlet compounds the curtains' effect and makes red more noticeable than yellow in the space. Similarly, a canopy crafted of gold fabric (opposite) makes a throne-like presence for a bed surrounded by yellow walls and draws the eye to it. The navy blue plaid duvet cover and canopy top create a cozy sense of enclosure around the bed.

The floral wallpaper and fabrics in vibrant pinks and reds in a dressing room (opposite) extend more than splashes of color; their rich graphic imagery imparts great drama. A gingham ottoman and throw pillows provide an interesting contrast to the floral fabrics — the rigid geometry and small scale of the checks balance the blossoms' lush nature — and show how color and pattern work together to establish the personality of a room. In a bedroom (above), the bed linens, wallpaper, and upholstery take their cue from the quilt and mix and match squares of different sizes to spread the friendly face of blue and white around the space. They prove that a variety of different fabrics can live well in a room if they are graphically linked and that a common pattern is one of the most powerful ways to communicate a color scheme.

Multicolored and patterned, quilts are excellent sources of color inspiration and introduce wide-ranging palettes, which other fabrics and rugs in a room can elaborate on. In a bedroom (opposite), three different colors of bed sheets, vinyl flooring featuring bold stripes, and floral pillows mirror the quilt's lovely colors. In a living room (above), three vintage quilts hung as drapes and a center swag set the stage for a variety of floral and plaid fabrics that energize a collection of 1920s furniture and sustain its nostalgic mood. The many patterns are harmonized by sporting the same colors as the quilts. In another bedroom (overleaf), a vibrant bed quilt featuring a strong fan motif presents a rainbow of color that is echoed in the striped upholstery fabric, the window swag, and the many different pillow fabrics. With the wealth of color the quilt provides, almost anything goes in this room. The upbeat peach tone of the walls reflects one of the colors in the quilt and ties together the various patterned fabrics.

SIMPLE GEOMETRY

Mixing patterns works best when there is a common denominator among them such as a specific color or motif. In one of country's most classic pattern pairings, checks and stripes share a sense of geometry. These two favorites form an even more dynamic partnership when they sport separate colors that affect a room's atmosphere in a similar way— such as yellow and red, both of which add cheerful flair, warmth, and vigor.

In a Craftsman-style cottage, fabrics in these traditional patterns not only forge bold graphic appeal but lend the rooms a casual air in keeping with the cozy scale of the cottage. In the living room, thick stripes covering a generous club chair combine with the crisscrossed stripes in a boldly checkered chaise longue and a pattern of thick and thin stripes in an area rug to lead the eye in multiple directions. These stripes are echoed by the vertical grooves in the armoire doors, the grid of the divided-light window, and the slatted base of the coffee table. The stunning effect of this layering of pattern, texture,

and warm color is a room that feels longer and higher than it actually is.

The interplay of color and pattern through fabric is repeated in the dining room on a built-in window seat and around a white pedestal dining table that lets the vividly dressed chairs hold center stage. The boldly checkered upholstery, the same fabric used on the chaise longue in the living room, picks up on the pale citrus wall color and is balanced by the red and white striped chairs placed along the perimeter of the room. In both rooms, throw pillows, on the wicker settee in the living room and on the window seat in the dining room, play up the happy meeting of color and pattern. They contain the colors — red and yellow plus blue — and the patterns — stripes and checks plus a plaid — that coexist so exuberantly in the room's other furnishings. These warm colors and graphic patterns deliver the enduring message that when a room feels comfortable, it is usually the result of a harmonious relationship both between the colors and the patterns in it.

BOUQUETS OF COLOR

F loral patterns are the most popular of prints. Indeed, entire industries have been created to support their popularity — Liberty of London, William Morris, and Laura Ashley come to mind. Floral fabrics create depth and dimension in interiors and offer rich colors that suggest carefree days and endless summers. The owner of an 1810 house in southwestern Connecticut selected two different floral chintzes to update and enliven a bedroom, lining the walls with one pattern and covering the window and a corner chaise longue with another coordinating one. The two fabrics work together to create an understated sophistication, in part because of what they have in common: a shared palette of rose, lavender, and green on a white background. A white background on fabric or wallpaper makes anything look larger, walls or furniture, and therefore more buoyant and airy. In concert, these fabrics create a field of dreams, a colorful nook in which to indulge favorite pastimes.

In the same way that blossoms can unify the diverse elements of an outdoor landscape, a floral fabric used repeatedly can harmonize a variety of decorative ingredients, from small porcelain dog statues to a collection of plates to wicker furniture, and transform a small space into one that feels larger and less choppy. The owner of a New York City apartment decorated the living room with slipcovers, curtains, pillows, and a table skirt made from a 1930s chintz pattern. The floral is displayed to its fullest glory, yet it is tempered by walls of pale slate blue, a neutral color found in small amounts in the floral. This choice of wall color keeps the print from being too sweet and feminine and makes it acceptable for a living room.

There is little that floral fabrics won't accommodate; their blossoms wrap rooms in bursts of color and spontaneity. These timeless patterns recall the charming cottages and brimming gardens of the English countryside and can be used in homes decorated in a range of styles from relaxed to formal.

In a bedroom (opposite), chintz-lined walls, window shade, and chaise longue fashion a corner full of rosy hues. A solid burgundy throw provides a place for the eye to rest among the many spots of brilliant color. In a small apartment (overleaf), a vintage floral chintz pattern that repeats throughout the living room transforms the compact space into a sweeping interior landscape with a garden-like quality.

DETAILS

If walls and furniture are the bones of a room, decorative accessories are its lifeblood. Without the arresting displays and splashes of color they provide, rooms can look unfinished and uninhabited. A still life painting hung like a celebrated masterwork over a stately sofa, a collection of gleaming glass vases placed on a mantel, a handmade quilt tossed over a wood table, a hooked rug laid on a foyer floor — these are the details that bring color and personality to a space. Whereas paint contributes color to surfaces and fabric extends color with the added allure of tactility, texture, and pattern, small objects have the distinct advantage of providing color in what is perhaps its most riveting package: fascinating forms and materials imbued with historical or sentimental significance.

Decorative accessories are often received as gifts or gathered over many years to shape special collections. Such details tell stories, and their narrative weight endows their colors with emotional value. Even a room framed by white walls and filled with white furniture will seem dressed in lively color if bold accessories dot its surfaces.

Lightweight and eminently portable, small objects are movable feasts for the eyes; they present an opportunity to change the look of a room quickly by shifting their place in a particular grouping or by moving the entire arrangement to a different location. Details are also the easiest way to lead color that appears in one part of a room to another part and thereby create a sense of movement through it. By playing a single detail or collection against wall colors or furniture tones it is possible to amplify their decorative power — picture, for example, blue dishware in a blue painted hutch or a green fire screen near a green wall. The wall and furniture look richer for the presence of the accents alongside them. Every bit of color a detail supplies is an open portal through which other items are welcomed into a home.

In a neutral setting, the eye roves about, lingering wherever vivid color appears. In a white room (opposite), color appears in splashes of pure primaries: framed pages of a children's book, glass vases on the mantel, and checkered upholstery trim. In another white living room (above), a sense of movement is created by a scattering of bright folk art pieces. On a wall of shelves (overleaf), books, green stoneware, and charming collectibles, artfully arranged, are notes of bright color in an otherwise all-white room.

In a dining room (above), a layering of quilts — a yellow quilt with a floral border over a deep red one backed with rich yellow — and an Oriental carpet make a table the victor in the visual competition that exists between the dining surface and the lovely view outside. Hot colors hook the eye more readily than cool ones: Earthy yellow urns filled with flowers that echo the quilt lift the color off the table and situate it strategically so that the green lawn becomes a soothing backdrop for a captivating interior. In a dining room where wood tones could dominate (opposite), green chairs with warmly colored chair pads and a red cabinet draw attention away from the wood. The table setting of matching green place mats and napkins in green's complementary color, a festive red, reinforces the dynamic created by a color scheme of complementary colors and softens the room's rustic character.

Rooms need one or more focal points, an architectural or decorative feature that anchors the space in color and form. A china collection is a wonderful way to evoke both history and personal memories in a room and build an island of color on a tabletop, in a hutch, or on a wall shelf. A grouping of brilliant yellow china (opposite) that boasts vivid red floral patterns shapes an eye-catching display. The piece of furniture that showcases a collection can enhance its beauty by featuring the colors that appear in it. The corner cupboard (above left) painted a vivid country blue is a perfect match for the Staffordshire china within. A cluster of hat boxes that sport the same color provides a crowning touch. The wall unit (above right) shows that just a few pieces of redware encased in opposing green, which highlights the plates' ruddy tones, provide a window of color on a white wall. A bowl of fresh fruit on the table reflects the golden and reddish tones of the plates.

A rug packs a lot of punch and grounds a room in both color and pattern. This base can transform a neutral setting into a decorative powerhouse if smaller accessories elaborate upon the color cues it offers. In a casual living room (above), a round rug and Amish quilt above the sofa shape an envelope of vibrant color echoed in the throw pillows, corner cabinet, and child's blocks on the painted chest that serves as a coffee table. The room appears red, but the secondary details — the blue chest, gray sofa, and beige woven side chair — tone down red's energy. In a more formal living room (opposite), an Oriental carpet joins a painted fire screen to serve as the prime color catalysts in a beige room. Following the fire screen's lead, the mantel and chair rail are painted a calming green, which balances the reds in the carpet and the reddish browns of the wood furnishings.

A FINAL TOUCH

When the owners of a contemporary house, built in the 1970s in Massachusetts, sought to lend their living room an Early American character, they commissioned a hand-painted decorative wall frieze on canvas, applied to the wall at the base of the second-floor balcony and continued around the entire room at this height. The color provided by the foliage pattern establishes a palette for the space that other accessories — from an early-nineteenth-century Bethlehem Star quilt to game boards and leaf-printed upholstery fabric — flesh out at eye level. The painted border prevents the eye from floating over the soaring expanses of neutral-colored walls by providing a strong visual component that it can latch on to. Though it divides the vertical space, the border underscores the soaring height by making it more friendly and visually digestible, and it calls attention to the repeating rhythm of the straight lines of the balcony and staircase balusters.

A similar effect can be achieved with the many ready-made wallpaper borders available in home design stores. These decorative borders make ideal accents at chair-rail height, at ceiling level, or along the baseboard. The patterns and colors they introduce can complement existing color and decorative schemes or serve as counterpoints for them. A border can repeat a wallpaper or fabric design used elsewhere in the room, highlight the color or pattern of a dominant design in the room, or provide a note of surprise by introducing an entirely new color or pattern to the existing decorating scheme.

In this house, the frieze complements the historical accessories but is also a warm and whimsical foil for the hard-edged industrial design collectibles the homeowners have gathered, such as the metal grate on the mantel and the iron trolley that functions as a coffee table.

Decorative trims are details that truly bring a room to life, especially in the absence of architectural moldings. They add resonance to a room, provide a focus for the eye, and allow for the witty expression of the homeowner's personality.

PHOTOGRAPHY CREDITS

1–21	Keith Scott Morton	132	Keith Scott Morton
24	Keith Scott Morton	133–134	Jessie Walker
26	Jessie Walker	135–146	Keith Scott Morton
27	Keith Scott Morton	147	*(top)* Jessie Walker *(bottom)* Keith Scott Morton
28	Peter Margonelli	148–151	Keith Scott Morton
29–30	Keith Scott Morton	153	Feliciano
31	Jessie Walker	154–165	Keith Scott Morton
32–33	John Vaughan	166	Jeremy Samuelson
34–44	Keith Scott Morton	167	*(top)* Jeremy Samuelson
46–47	Kari Haavisto	167	*(bottom)* Keith Scott Morton
48	Feliciano	168–171	Keith Scott Morton
49–53	Keith Scott Morton	172	Al Teufen
54	Jessie Walker	173	Kari Haavisto
55	Keith Scott Morton	174–186	Keith Scott Morton
56–57	Jessie Walker	188	Jessie Walker
58–64	Keith Scott Morton	190–193	Keith Scott Morton
67–71	Jessie Walker	194	Steven Mays
74–89	Keith Scott Morton	195–201	Keith Scott Morton
90	Jessie Walker	202	Jessie Walker
91	*(left)* Keith Scott Morton *(right)* Jessie Walker	205–214	Keith Scott Morton
93–105	Keith Scott Morton	215	Michael Dunne
106–107	John Vaughan	216	Keith Scott Morton
108–113	Keith Scott Morton	217	*(left)* Jessie Walker *(right)* Keith Scott Morton
114	Jessie Walker	218–222	Keith Scott Morton
115–128	Keith Scott Morton	224	Jessie Walker
129–131	Jessie Walker		

COUNTRY LIVING WOULD LIKE TO THANK

THE MANY HOMEOWNERS, DESIGNERS, AND ARCHITECTS

WHOSE WORK APPEARS ON THESE PAGES.